Foreword

Cllr Jagdish Sharma MBE

W hen Keith Vaz first approached
Hounslow Council in the Summer of
1994, we were daunted by the task
offered us to complete: to hold the
first-ever National Convention for Black, Asian and
Ethnic Minority Councillors without, at first, any
substantial commitments in terms of administrative and
financial resources.

The fact that, eight months later, we were host to
nearly half of all the Black, Asian and Ethnic Minority
Councillors in Britain, is testimony to the hard work
and endurance of the Convention's Steering
Committee. *It shows what can be done if we are united in a
common purpose.*

It was a challenge faced and a challenge overcome.
In many respects, Black, Asian and Ethnic Minority
Councillors all over the country are faced with
challenges. Not only will many of us be the only
'Black' or 'Asian' face in the Council, but we are often
put in the position of having to be the spokesperson on
Race Equality.

So what are the challenges for Race Equality in

Local Government as we approach the next millennium? This report is deliberately provocative and challenging in getting you to think about that Agenda for Race Equality. It also shares and values the experiences we can gain from the United States.

Our task, after reading this report, is to ensure it does not remain in a Council archive to be dusted down. It should be used

throughout this nation to empower Black, Asian and Ethnic Minority Councillors and to be used as the basis for organising real and lasting advancements for all the communities we serve.

I hope you will join the Steering Committee in our next 'challenge', to solidify the spirit of unity at the Convention, by seeking to establish a National Association for Black, Asian and Ethnic Minority Councillors. I hope together we can take up this challenge.

Cllr Jagdish Sharma MBE
Deputy Leader of Hounslow Council
Member of the Convention Steering Committee

Introduction

Keith Vaz MP

C an I, on behalf of the Members of the Steering Committee, welcome you to the Convention. I am pretty excited about this event because when we first thought of this idea last year it was difficult to imagine how many people would come to an event of this kind.

I want to begin by thanking the London Borough of Hounslow. As we looked at the map of Britain to find the Council that we thought was most suitable to be working on this project, Hounslow came to mind for two reasons: first of all because it has a good record in promoting policies we would all support, and secondly because it is totally unflashy, it doesn't go out and do dramatic things, it doesn't necessarily court the media, it gets on with its work in a quiet and efficient way. The fact that you have got half the number of Black, Asian and Ethnic Minority Councillors ever in British history shows that the work that Hounslow has done should be appreciated. I want to thank Jagdish Sharma and Members of the Council for allowing us to work with your officers, especially Bob Kerslake, Munira Thobani and Darryl Telles, in organising this event, because it has not been easy and it has taken a whole year to bring to fruition.

I also want to thank those who took part in the Steering Group. How did we choose the Steering Group? Well, we tried to get a geographical balance, a balance in all kinds of ways so that everyone would think it was representative and no-one would quarrel with it. We came across a group of people who worked together so effectively, I was amazed how well they all got on! They were Jagdish Sharma from Hounslow, Muhammad Afzal from Birmingham, Councillor Mee Ling Ng from Lewisham, Lester Holloway from Hammersmith and Fulham, Councillor Rajinder Sohpal from Reading, Councillor Narendra Makanji from Haringey, Councillor Nirmal Roy from Camden and Councillor Joe Allen from Leicester.

This event is an all party event. Before our speakers begin I shall be reading out greetings from Tony Blair, John Major and Paddy Ashdown and I want you to reflect on how many events you can go to in local government where you get good wishes from those three gentlemen!

We have others from all political parties here today. You do not know who the Tories are or who the Labour people are; we haven't identified you because we're here for a particular purpose. We're here to see whether this gathering will be the one and only gathering of Black, Asian and Ethnic Minority Councillors or if it will be the first of many gatherings to come. I hope it will be the latter, but it's very much in *your* hands because all that the Steering Group has

done and all that Hounslow has done is to
try and steer it in a particular direction to
make sure the event takes place. I suppose
the first thing we should all congratulate
ourselves upon from wherever we come –
West Glamorgan, Kirklees, Glasgow or
Hampshire – is the fact that you've come
all this way to be here today and the fact
that we're holding this particular
Convention.

KEITH VAZ MP

This is not a policy making Convention
– we cannot make policy. I know people
will have their own particular views on the political
parties but it is not a party political event as such. I
hope we will raise issues that we are going to be able to
take on as elected representatives because I believe we
are all colleagues together, *we share the same experience
and the same expectations.*

The reason we have decided to have this event is
because of the American experience and that is why
I'm so delighted that Congressman Frazer is here.
American Black political advancement is well ahead of
what we have achieved in Britain. There are so many
examples of the collective nature in which Black
elected officials come together in order to pursue
particular aims. At Congress there is a Congressional
Black Caucus which, until the Republicans took
control, had a veto on government policy. The 40 or so
Black Congressmen could actually determine the
policy of the American administration. President
Clinton has appointed high profile Black people to his

cabinet. At a local level there are collections of Governors of States, of Mayors and of Assembly people, so there is a potential for us to learn from that experience.

My main regret is that in Parliament in Britain we weren't able, for a variety of reasons, to do what you are all doing today, which is come together as a Black Caucus and work together in order to discuss issues of concern. That is one of the great failures of the last eight years but I hope that looking at what they have done in America will allow you to do something similar.

What I hope we will do, apart from obviously being nice to each other, is not to concentrate on personalities but rather to concentrate on issues and learn from each other's experiences.

More is expected of us than anybody else.

As we approach the millennium, *networking* for us is of great importance. All of you are very special because you will have achieved enormous things in your own local areas. You are either the first Black or Asian or Ethnic Minority Councillors in your areas or you're the first Chair of a particular Committee or you're the first Mayor or the first Deputy Leader, you're the first something. So each one of you has achieved an enormous amount in the work you have done and therefore your experience is important, but it is important not on its own but as a shared experience with others and we need to be able to make sure that that experience is networked. I was talking to a colleague from one of the London Boroughs who is the only Asian Councillor in that London Borough and he was saying he wanted the support of others because he wanted to know what the pitfalls were. *I could write a book about the pitfalls of being an MP* and I'm sure all of you could write similar things about what's happened to you – but it's that networking that is of crucial importance.

I remember getting a call from the first Black Chief Whip from one of our Metropolitan Councils. She had just been elected and she needed support and guidance as to how she could get through, not to find out what to do as a Chief Whip, but how to get through to the switchboard at Walworth Road, which was a major problem for anyone as you all know. So networking is the first theme.

The second theme is *support*. The ability of all of us in different parts of the country to be able to support each other because of our common experience. Out there is a hostile world. As all of you know, people expect from us – because of the colour of our skins – much higher standards than they expect from white elected officials. You all know that. They expect you to work harder. They expect you to deliver more. They expect you to be constantly, constantly, at the disposal of not just your electorate, but also the community. *More is expected of us than anybody else.*

Part of the problems that Ron Brown is going through in America is not because he happens to be the Secretary of Commerce but, I believe, because he happens to be *Black* and the first senior Black official. I know this may be unpopular in some circles, but I think some of the problems that Winnie Mandela is being put through by the media in this country is just because she happens to be a Black woman. And the leader writers of the *Independent* and the *Guardian*, when they write their columns, as they do, should try and remember the experiences of fighting apartheid before they start condemning Black people, whoever they are, over what they have been through.

The last main theme I hope we pick up is the theme of *organisation. You can be the most wonderful politician in the world, but if you are not organised then, frankly, you cannot make a success of what you are trying to achieve.*

We all build our local coalitions. Whether we are MPs or Councillors in our own areas. Sometimes we become the prisoner of those coalitions, but we have to be organised because there is an enormous amount of power out there. I hope, as we get through to the selections in Parliament this year and those in four years time, that we are going to have more Black, Asian and Ethnic Minority people elected to Parliament. I hope that will happen. I know it is going to be enormously difficult. Diane will tell you the same as I will tell you: if we hadn't been elected in 1987, I don't think we could have been selected to stand again for Parliament. We have Ashok Kumar, who is sitting in the audience, who stood in a seat in Middlesbrough where there were hardly any Black or Asian people and he got elected in a by-election. And it's awful to be a by-election candidate as the struggle that you have to go through is enormous. We want to make sure people are supported to achieve that again.

> *You can be the most wonderful politician in the world, but if you are not organised, then frankly, you cannot make a success of what you are trying to achieve.*

We want to make sure we have Black, Asian and Ethnic Minority leaders of Councils, Deputy leaders of Councils and Chairs of major committees. There is no reason for anyone to feel that they are going to be excluded. *The power is there. One needs to organise in order to exercise it efficiently.*

Finally let me say this. *All of you here today know this will not be on the Nine O'clock News. It will not be on the front page of the **Guardian** tomorrow. But they will miss a very historic event that's taking place today.* It is a pioneering event and all of you are present at the ground breaking process. Each one of you I believe has a responsibility to make sure this organisation works and it can work.

And I believe with the talent that we see around this room you should make sure that it will work. And the way in which you can do that is to ensure that it best reflects the real talent that exists out there, it does not become a prisoner of a particular faction but it represents everybody in the most effective way that will put our views forward. Thank you for coming. I hope you have a very successful day.

Our first keynote speaker is Congressman Victor Frazer. Congressman Frazer represents the Virgin Islands in the United States Congress. He is only the second native Virgin Islander to be elected to the US House of Representatives. After graduation from Charlotte School in 1960 he attended Fisk University in Nashville, Tennessee and graduated in 1964 with a Bachelors Degree in History. He spent from 1964 to 1968 working in banking at Hanover Trust Company in New York City and the Security Trust Company in Rochester, New York. In 1968, Mr. Frazer entered Howard University School of Law in Washington DC and was awarded a Doctorate in 1971.

Congressman Frazer has worked for several members of the US Congress since 1981. He has served as Counsel to the committee in the district of Columbia and the sub-committee on Judiciary Education. He worked on the staff of Congressman John Conyers of Michigan. He was instrumental in the creation of the Caribbean Action Lobby, which lobbies on behalf of the other Caribbean Islands.

Sharing the US Experience

Congressman Victor Frazer

Thank you. It's an unexpected privilege for me to be here with you. We speak about political involvement. I guess you recognise that Blacks were not involved in any kind of political activity in the United States until after the Civil War. As a matter of fact, at that time we were not even people. We were considered 3/5 of a person. I don't know what parts were missing – the arms or the legs. I never quite understood why it is that the Constitution officially listed Blacks as 3/5 of a person. I don't know when we gained the other 2/5 but somehow these days we are considered full people. So now we are no longer chattel and we are permitted to be here as though we are real. Reconstruction, as you know, was that period after the Civil War: the Great War between the States, the war to liberate the slaves. Quite a misnomer as you know. It was a war to keep the Union intact. The fact that the slaves were liberated was an afterthought. As Mr Lincoln himself said 'the purpose for pursuing the war was not to liberate slaves, but to keep the Union intact'. The fact that we got liberated was an aside to all benefit and we really don't care for his motive. We are

CONGRESSMAN
VICTOR FRAZER

now liberated and we are happy for that. At the end of the Civil War the victorious North, in an attempt to keep the South in check and I suppose to make sure that it wouldn't raise its ugly head again trying to separate the Union, encouraged Black participation in the electoral process. It is funny, it is strange to learn that during that period before 1871 there were more Blacks in Congress in a short period of time than any other time in the history of politics in the United States. But what happened twenty years later was the States started coming about with new laws to their constitutions that almost prohibited Black participation in national politics. But strangely enough all of the Blacks involved in politics after Reconstruction were members of the Republican party because that was the party of Lincoln the great emancipator. So I guess naturally Blacks gravitated towards that side of the aisle. However, between 1870 and 30 years after, the States set about disenfranchising Blacks. It was a 30 year period in which there were no members in Congress. Rather strange that you suddenly had no members in Congress, when 20 years prior you had members in the House and in the Senate. But again those who would like to remain in charge spend hours, they spend their waking hours, making sure that so-called minorities don't advance. *While we are asleep counting our gains they are trying to make sure that they are eroded.* And this is exactly what happened.

As members of the Congress of the United States

when segregation was legal, you had Black members of
the House and the Senate who were still segregated.
They couldn't travel from their district to Washington
in stagecoach or cars with the other members. They
were segregated even within the capital of the United
States. So you see, segregation appeared to be natural. I
guess it's only natural if it's a natural phenomenon in
nature. But when it is used to work against people who
have been disenfranchised I don't think it's natural. I
think it's contrived and planned.

The history of the Congressional Black Caucus
starts from 1971. In 1971 there were 13 Black members
in the House of Representatives and of course they had
a common constituency - the Blacks of the United
States. In spite of the fact that there were only 13
members, every Black in the United States considered
those members were their representatives. Obviously it
was expected that if we were now members of
Congress every Black person in Congress should
pursue the interests of Black people of the United
States and this is what happened. However, because of
the small number the strength was rather limited. But
again, even though segregation was no longer legal,
disrespect for Black members continued.

The first time the Caucus, after formation, tried to
have a meeting with the President, then Richard
Nixon, he refused. Another slap in the face. I guess
even though we considered ourselves members of the
House, he considered us a minority. We often forget
who we are. We look at what we wear, what we have
achieved, the degrees we have acquired and we think

*While we are asleep
counting our gains
they are trying to
make sure that they
are eroded.*

that we have somehow left the group. But it never happens *because all you need to do is look in the mirror and you recognise you are still part of the group.* A police officer stops you in a major American city. The fact that you are a Harvard Law Graduate and you may have been to Oxford or Cambridge is totally irrelevant, he sees a Black face. What you see in your mind is your degrees and your position but that is totally irrelevant to him.

If more of us continue to remember what we are rather than what we think we are, we wouldn't really have these problems.

The Congressional Black Caucus wrestled with what they would call themselves, whether they would call themselves the "Black Members of Congress" or "Black Representatives to Washington". In the end, they decided to call themselves the "Congressional Black Caucus Members of Congress". But even in the title there was a problem because again it was viewed that these Members had one agenda which was the agenda of Black people. That wasn't the case, because Congressional Black members come from districts where they have people of all races. But because traditionally the interests of Black people had not been pursued in the Congress of the United States, it was important to have people that looked like Black people in Congress, people who didn't have to be told what the problems of Blacks were; we knew it instinctively. Of course there are those of us who tend to forget what the problems are. But I think when we close our doors at night we do recognise that we are still part of that group. The Caucus tried to bring to the forefront

...all you need to do is look in the mirror and you recognise you are still part of the group.

of the national agenda those issues that had been
ignored by the majority Representation in the
Congress of the United States.

Black people's problems are unique. We have for the
most part been ignored in the agenda. *We have been
viewed as a second thought, sometimes as a necessary
inconvenience to be dealt with.* Hopefully we would sit in
the back row and not make a lot of trouble and when
we do we get branded. For fear of that, many of us sit
in audiences and stay quiet. We recognise the wrongs
that are being done to us, and we often blame the
victims for what happens to them. If I get on a bus and
there's a Black fellow on there making a nuisance of
himself – everybody white looks at me wondering what
I am going to do about it? Why is that fellow behaving
like this? If I get on a bus and there is a white fellow
making a nuisance of himself, everybody ignores him
and says he's on his own. These are the kind of
obstacles that we face when we try to work within the
confines of a major community or society which has
ignored us and not given us our rightful place, often
saying to us we have no place in this country. This is
not our country, this is America – as though the whites
we find in the United States are the natives of that
country.

They have called native Americans by various names
– Indian Apaches and otherwise – rather than the
'natives' of that country. They speak of us as foreigners
or immigrants and, when we raise our heads protesting
their treatment of us, they invite us to go back home to
Africa. If I invite them to go back home to England or

> *We have been viewed as a second thought, sometimes as a necessary inconvenience to be dealt with.*

France or elsewhere, my statement will be viewed as seditious because America belongs to the Americans and that means whites. The Indians, in fact, are also immigrants, I guess, from somewhere else.

But they know the truth. And the truth is not to be told in public. It is for us to believe that America belongs to the Americans and the Blacks are interlopers.

The influence of the members of the American Black Caucus grew as their numbers grew, and the seniority system in the Congress of the United States is the most important aspect of longevity in the Congress. You move up the ladder through seniority and you get major Committees. I guess many of you know the name Adam Clayton Powell. He stayed in Congress, as far as the white majority was concerned, too long because he became the powerful chairman of the Old House Education and Labour Committee and that's where his troubles began.

He was too powerful and something had to be done to put him in his place. There were whites who had engaged in worse behaviour than Adam. But of course the standards were theirs. He was supposed to be chastised and put in his place. So everything was done to remove him from that Committee and ultimately he was removed. But in spite of that, his own people in Harlem re-elected him and his colleagues and Congress refused to seat him, even though there were no provisions in the Constitution for that. *Again, when you are playing in a game where somebody else made the rules, and when you have learned the rules well enough to beat him at his own game, he changes the rules.*

We have several Black organisations in the United States that come together as you have done today. And I do hope this is the first. I hope you will do it again next year. And I hope that the Caucus will again be invited and more of us would come.

I am not here representing myself, but I am here representing the Congressional Black Caucus, the Black people of the United States who would like to network, who know that there are Blacks in this country. We read the paper, we look at the TV and we recognise that you are going through what we have gone through for several hundred years. We hope that somehow we could share with you our own experiences and that from that you can go on and find some way of resolving the problems that you are now facing. We have somehow become experts at facing problems.

We also have a National Black Leadership round table where Black leaders from business, government and otherwise come together every year to discuss issues relevant to Black people. We also have a National Black Caucus of local elected officials, such as this. Again, in spite of the fact that you have come from various parts of the country, I am sure that your constituency being similar you experience the same problems. And I think it is important to *share* problems with each other. *Rather than everybody trying to reinvent the wheel. Let us all try to roll the same wheel down the same street*, sharing with you proposals for a solution to common problems.

There is also the National Black Caucus of State Legislators. If your question is why we have so many Caucuses, it's because we have so many levels of Government. It's important that Blacks in the United States come together from various levels within the Government. Again, the Congressional Black Caucus, as you would view it in a hierarchy, is the highest elected office in the United States.

I guess the next is President and we are still looking at that. But I am sure there are those at the gate who have decided that it will be some time to come. Yet we always have Jesse Jackson to remind them that our aspirations are still intact.

Networking is very important. And it's important that you recognise that what you have to say is important to somebody else. The fact that you know it doesn't mean that it is widely known or widely held. You have to share your information with others. And as part of the network it's difficult to represent people if you are out of touch with them. You can't represent California from Washington DC. You could pursue the people's interests in Washington but you've got to go back

home to find out what it is they are concerned about. Because if you don't see your representative and he says that he's representing you, but you have not told him the issues that concern you, you should ask him what is it that he is doing. If he can't answer then you should appoint somebody else or you should invite

him to find another line of work. *It is important to go
back home and find out what the people who sent you to work
on their behalf are interested in. If you don't they are not
being served, you are not serving them, you ought to go home
yourself.*

I have been asked also to speak about an area called
affirmative action. Affirmative action was supposed to
be an attempt to give disadvantaged, socially
disadvantaged, underprivileged and disenfranchised
people in the United States an ability to compete on
the level of everybody else. As a matter of fact, in terms
of football or baseball or any other sport, it was to level
the field. Of course, the ones who are on the upside of
that incline decided it was wrong because they were
now going to be discriminated against. Well the
question was how do we level the field if we don't
bring your side of the incline down and raise the other.
But it wasn't fair they said because they discriminated
against us to undo a former discrimination. I don't
know any other way of making things level if you don't
attack the discrimination in the past. How would you
ever get those people who were disenfranchised to a
level to compete. They will never be at that level to
compete to begin with, because the majority have had
generations and years of privilege. Now they are crying
that others are going to enjoy those same privileges.
And it's wrong. The people in the United States today
that are crying the loudest are white men because you
know power means white men and I don't think it's
just restricted to the United States. *I think that white men
believe that somehow somebody came down from heaven or*

> *...as part of the
> network it's difficult
> to represent people if
> you are out of touch
> with them.*

elsewhere of great authority, and said, "this world is yours".

It's not a difficult thing to get white men to believe that they should be in charge. And they hate to see anyone else approach such a level of importance or competence. It's very difficult to pull yourself up by the bootstraps when you don't have boots but you're expected to do it anyway. And this is what White people are doing. I would hate anyone to leave here today and say that I came over here blasting Whites. As long as we call ourselves Black I will call them White because this is what I have often heard.

The problems that Blacks have had in a political arena relate to political power – because Blacks don't have political power. Blacks have a growing political awareness and a growing political influence but not power, because Blacks and power are not supposed to go together. There was a time in the 60s when Black power was a word to be used, but not Blacks and power. The first problem that I find that Blacks have in the political arena is money. It's a bad word. Nobody wants to use it. You have a limitation on spending here we don't have in the United States. What has happened is that money has become so important that Blacks have been for the most part left out of the political arena. *It takes money to run a campaign.* Last year we had someone in California that spent $28 million of his own money. $28 million for a seat in the Senate, and he lost!

And when we say to them, "We need money to run campaigns", many of them say that if you want to be in politics you'll find a way of raising the money. But you

> *Blacks have a growing political awareness and a growing political influence, but not power...*

FACING THE CHALLENGE

need money. As a personal experience, I ran a
campaign last year out of pocket. Money has always
been the biggest hindrance to Black political
involvement. Another one is gerrymandering.
Reapportionment it's called. When Blacks start going up
the political ladder, suddenly there needs to be
apportionment.

We'll draw the lines differently. So we would take a
Black majority district into the white district. Now not
only can white money be used against you but White
votes.

One of the things that we have to look forward to is
*the fact that when our powers appear to rise the other side is
steadily at work to chop them down.*

We have a history of distrust of each other. For so
long we believed that our interests would be pursued
by white elected officials. That hasn't been the case. We
have a history of believing that our place is at the
bottom. In the United States in particular it is a vestige
of slavery. We have been indoctrinated over centuries
into believing that we are nobodies, and many of us
believe that we are nobodies. We are quick to believe
the worst of each other. And I don't think it's restricted
to us in the United States and that is a hindrance.
Because we have been told that's how it is. And I think
it's time that we start thinking otherwise.

We as Black people have got to understand that we
do not exist in a vacuum. Whether it's in England,
India, the Virgin Islands or Washington DC the
problems are the same. We are thought of as being
interlopers and foreigners, we are thought of as not

having a right to be here, and it is something that we must fight against every day.

So, you have to build coalitions. If we want to do those things on behalf of the people we represent, our own constituency, we must form *coalitions*. But the drawback to that is that the people we represent look at that very suspiciously. They say if you are talking to members of the clan you may have sold out. We're just trying to make sure that we remain in the game. *It's more important to be in the game than to be outside.* But, these are the things that we come up against – political apathy – and it's easily understood. We as a people have never had a history of being politically powerful so we become politically apathetic. We say what's the point? What difference does it make? It makes a difference, because a little difference is better than no difference at all. Don't be suspicious of coalition building – it's necessary. Explain to the folks back home what you are doing. People like to know what is happening. They're not as suspicious of you, even if you're pursuing matters on people's behalf – in their better interest. If they don't know, they're suspicious. You are better to tell your constituents what it is you do and why it is you do it. You don't lead from the back of the column you lead from in front, not just by talk but by action. It's important when you represent people that you're you, as their representative, not as somebody who's taken that position to advertise yourself.

I looked at your British Race Relations Act and I looked at it again last night because I had hoped that perhaps I had missed something. But again last night I

> *It's more important to be in the game than to be outside.*

saw the same tiger that had visited his dentist. The
Race Relations Act, I guess, has some relevance but I
don't know if it has teeth. I remember the Civil Rights
Act of 1964. That was an attempt in the United States
to give some semblance of recognition of the rights of
Black Americans. Some semblance!

I thought your Race Relations Act was exactly
what it says: some attempt to bring the races together,
an attempt at parity. And in all honesty, I read it twice
but I didn't find it to be so. It was, it appeared to be, an
elementary approach to saying to folks who have been
dissatisfied, "Things are going to get better". But I
guess I'm still waiting to see when it does.

The Affirmative Action Programme in the United
States was an attempt as we said earlier to level the
field. Because it's important that if you are going to say
you're equal, at least let it appear that we are. But as a
result of the Affirmative Action Programme there's
been a backlash.

Suddenly we find courts being filled with cases
brought by white men who are now saying they have
been disadvantaged.

That's just not the case. We know it's not the case.
They are trying to turn back the clock by saying, "We
have been discriminated against". The purpose was to
bring the disadvantaged up to par. It happened and it
got rolled back.

The Federal Government in it's procurement
practises said, "We will set aside a portion of every
major project beyond $50,000 for minorities".

What has happened? You found white companies

going out and getting minorities 'Blacks' to front their businesses.

Every time there is a law to give minorities or Blacks in the United States some parity, the devil is awake at night finding some way to roll it back. So now there is a current backlash in the United States against this Affirmative Action. Affirmative Action/Positive Action – the rights of everyone to have a chance. A chance at what? A chance to compete fairly. It doesn't happen. I am not being pessimistic. I'm not throwing my hands up in the air and saying, "Life will not get better". *It is just that every time we take one step forward, it seems as though somebody has pulled the walkway back.* So the tree that you thought you were parallel with is suddenly 10ft ahead of you again. I notice in major cities across Europe, and yes also in the United States, fascism and racism. And in economical hard times, what do you do? You point back at the foreigners who have been working hard and who have appeared to have achieved something and said, "They are responsible for my lot". It's easy to do.

You're Indians, you're West Indians, you're Africans, you've worked hard. Somebody white didn't go to school or went to school and fell asleep, dropped out. Whatever he did. So now he blames us. Racism seems to be at it's highest in economic hard times. It's happening in the United States. I read the paper and I see it's happening across Europe. *What do you do about it? Continue to fight. You don't look the other way and say "It didn't happen to me" because in time it will happen to you.* And if you keep looking back at the group you

> *It is just that everytime we take one step forward, it seems as though somebody has pulled the walkway back.*

will consider that anything that happened to the group, happened to you.

Let us not delude ourselves into believing that we've arrived. Because we may have arrived, but we are at the wrong destination.

As long as we have a Black or other coloured face, we will be viewed as part of a minority,

irrespective of our numbers. Somebody white comes into the room and we're still the minority. I don't know why it is. I thought the minority was indicated by numbers but somehow it seems to be race. Even in the Virgin Islands where Blacks live in larger numbers, for the purposes of Federal procurement we are again called a 'minority'. And I question that. I say "Are we the minority in numbers? No. Then why are we the minority?" Well this is how the statute's written. We'll rewrite the statute. Something is definitely wrong.

I hope that the experience we have had in the Congress of the United States, that we have had in the United States as Black people, will somehow give you a picture of how we approach those problems. I would hope that the history the Caucus has brought to the forefront would somehow give you some proposed solution to the same problems. Problems are the same. And as we speak of legislative involvement it is important that legislators, at any level, network. And that what is called the City Council, Province or the

Borough, that they don't deal only within the confines of their own responsibility but that they go as high as the Parliament. There must be more Blacks, Indians, West Indians, Africans and others sitting in Parliament. It is going to be because you and others like you have reached up and said it is possible and that we are here somehow as pathfinders making a way. Don't sit there with those members who feel that it's their birthright without believing that it's your birthright also.

I said earlier I hope that this Convention, this Conference, is not viewed as an interlude from regular business and that folks here are all dressed up meeting each other and saying, what a wonderful time we have had, what a wonderful way to close the week. I don't know if we got time off work to be here, but this is what happens in many conventions that we have.

No one is going to make life better for us, but us. Nobody with power is going to share his power with you. I am not saying that you stick a gun in his back. But I am saying that it is important that we become aware of our right to be politically involved. If we convince students, young people, of their right to question authority and of their right to question those laws under which they live, they start believing these rights. And when they become adults and the first time that it is legally possible for them to register to vote, they will. Then you wouldn't have 30% of your population beyond the age of registration who've never registered.

In the last election, 38% of the American people voted. 38% changed the Congress of the United States. For 40 years the Democrats were in charge. Today they

> *No one is going to make life better for us, but us. Nobody with power is going to share his power with you.*

are not. Complacency. They took it for granted that
they would always be in charge. They did not go out
and prune their gardens. They did not weed, they
expected the vines to always yield fruits without any
attention. It doesn't happen like that. It's important to
recognise the need to always be on guard. The
watchman who falls asleep – he harms the entire
village. And as elected officials we should be viewed as
watchmen for the village. It's a responsibility that we
have. We should take it seriously. We have been
entrusted with people's lives, we should take that
seriously. It's a charge for which many of us come
willingly. I have been questioned since day one. I have
been expected to do much more in the three months
that I have been there than my white predecessor did in
twenty years. But the advantage that I have, in spite of
the fact that I was recently elected, is that I had worked
in the institution for twelve years. I am literally four
doors away from where I worked for ten years. So we
understand the institution and it's important that in
your elective positions you started bringing people into
your offices in turns on a volunteer basis. For as more
people understand the process, the better it is for us to
disseminate information to our communities.

Let us start getting out of the offices and going back
to the people who elected us so that they can see that
their representation is real. That's what is important.
Ivory towers are nice. It's a warm feeling – but they are
not real. Because if you look out of the window of
your ivory tower you see a disgruntled hoard below.

Ladies and gentlemen, every distinguished person

here, again, I thank you for this privilege of being here, a most unexpected privilege. I am here on behalf of the Congressional Black Caucus and in a way on behalf of Black people in the United States and the Virgin Islands. *I do hope that you keep the fire that you have started today going and if we can throw some gasoline on it somewhere along the way, we are prepared to do so.* If in fact you would wish to come to the United States to continue this I would personally make whatever provision is necessary and spread the word about what is happening in London.

Again, let me stake some claim to some British heritage – I have a right to do so. My parents are both native of Tortolin, the British Virgin Islands and I possess the status of belonger which permits me to go in and out without going through immigration. So I have some nexus to being here. But we in the Congress of the United States have this ongoing network with the Bundestag and with the Japanese Parliament and many other legislative bodies. Two weeks ago I was privileged to have in my office the entire women's coalition or Caucus from the Burundi Parliament and they were starving for information on the process. After two hours I had other appointments but they were not ready to leave because they were constantly turning pages and taking notes. So we spent most of the day with them. I was told through their interpreters that they were very pleased with the audience. But they could not have been pleased as much as I had been pleased for having the privilege of sharing with them our legislative experience and if in fact anything that I

have said today has given you some insight as to what
we have done to gain some political power, I am glad.
No one in this room could be happier than I for the
privilege of having been here and with breathless
anticipation I await your next invitation.

Sharing the UK Experience

Diane Abbott MP

I t's a great pleasure to be here on this platform. Like
everybody else I was riveted and enthralled by
Congressman Frazer's speech. It's a particular
pleasure to be on a platform with my colleague and
friend Keith Vaz who, many of you will know, recently
became the father of a little boy, Luke Vaz. So the
dynasty goes on! It's very difficult to follow the
contribution of the comrade from the United States,
but I wanted to perhaps talk a little bit about the
British experience.

What is interesting is how many parallels there are
between the British and the US experience. But the
first thing I want to say, and it's something I always say,
is that when we are talking about where we are now, in
1995, as Black and Asian politicians, we should always
be mindful of what we have contributed to this society.
It is only too common, in discussions in our Councils,
in discussions in Parliament, in discussions in the
media, to talk about Black and Asian people as if we are
a social problem – as if we are some difficulty. And
what it is always important to stress is that we as Black
and Asian people have contributed historically to this

society and continue to contribute. *We have helped build this society.*

When we talk about our political agenda and when we talk about what we want, what we want for the future of our communities and for our children's future, we do not come begging. We come for what is our right. *Whether it is the wealth from slavery which helped to build the society* and to which each and every one of our foreparents and grandparents helped to contribute, or whether it's the work of Black and Asian people after the Second World War rebuilding this country's Health Service, rebuilding this country's industry, this country's retail industry, we have contributed, and we should stand tall as politicians and as Black and Asian people when we come to debate our community with this society. Sadly it was only really in the mid '70s and early '80s that you started to see Black representation on local authorities in any numbers. In some ways, the process reached its height in the late '80s where, on the one hand, you had large numbers of Black and Asian Councillors up and down the country and, on the other hand, you had large and well funded race units and community units able to implement policies. It seemed as if things were going our way. It seemed as if there were grounds for optimism. But each one of you, I am sure, whatever local authority you come from, have seen in recent years a backlash against the advances we were able to make in the '80s.

All across the country units have been closed, posts have been lost, grants have been slashed. Our communities have suffered and it was never more

timely that we as Black and Asian politicians of all parties come together not only to share with our colleagues across the Atlantic but also to share with each other.

What is our concrete agenda for the rest of the decade in order to actually improve and advance our communities and to make our contribution to this society? The first thing I want to say to you, you will know already. I was a Councillor. I was elected to Westminster Council in 1982-1986 and my experience as a Councillor will be all of your experience as a Councillor. That somehow when these people get a Black politician, they expect ten times more from you than they expected from the white person they had before. Ten times more.

When I was a Councillor in Paddington I had community groups in my ward and they never saw my white council colleagues from one year end to another. But if they didn't see me one month, it was Diane what's happened to you? Where have you been? And so we start from a position, as Black and Asian politicians, where we are expected, I think, to perform earlier on. *There are more pressures put on us than on our white colleagues.* And there is an expectation that you will perform, from day one, whereas everybody knows it takes years to make an experienced Councillor who is able to deliver.

So we start from a position where we are facing a

backlash and where more is expected of us.

I think the first aspect of our agenda has to be an *economic* agenda. Because you know there was a danger, in recent years, that we allowed ourselves as politicians to get side-tracked and take our eye off the ball. The most crucial thing for us and our communities is economic security and well being. So we as Black and Asian politicians must not allow ourselves to be sidelined - on to this Race Committee, or that Race Working Party. I sit on the Treasury and Civil Service Select Committee of the House of Commons. I question the Governor of the Bank of England, The Chancellor of the Exchequer - because I believe that these economic issues are just as much my business as a Black person as for any white person. And the first thing that we have to be clear about in framing an agenda as Black and Asian politicians, regardless of party, is that we are in the mainstream. *We want to concern ourselves with mainstream issues,* particularly these mainstream economic issues.

We need to be concerning ourselves with the *employment* prospects for Black and Asian people and the promotion of Black and Asian people within our Authorities. Not just within the Race Unit but within the Authority as a whole. And of course, you will find, if you stand up at a Policy and Resources meeting and ask these questions about what's happening about employment and promotion, you will not be popular. But let me tell you, in case you don't know. *To be an effective Black and Asian politician is not always to be popular.*

So we start from a position where we are facing a backlash and where more is expected of us.

We have to be prepared to monitor what is happening in terms of *business development and support for Black business.* Because if we don't do it no one else is going to do it.

Just let me give you an example. When the Bank of Credit and Commerce International collapsed with tragic results for many people in the community and many businesses, let me tell you who was the person who took up this issue first and persisted with it until Members and Labour Shadows had to respond - Keith Vaz. Let me tell you because you know sometimes people don't understand. Keith Vaz took up this issue. Not just the Government wasn't interested but, quite frankly, my own front bench, the Labour Party, weren't interested. He took it up. He persisted with it, he made it a national issue and he did his best for the community. And so you know, we have to be there in the centre of these issues. We have to be prepared to take on the essential issues to do with our communities' livelihood whether or not it makes us popular, whether or not people like us for it. Because if we allow ourselves to be shuffled off into some sub-committee or working party or if we allow ourselves to be bought off with some meaningless Vice Chairmanship, what use are we? It's all too easy as a Black and Asian politician, to allow yourself to be sidelined, to allow yourself to be marginalized, to be bought off. Now I'm not saying that people shouldn't be bought off. But at what price? *I'm not saying that Tony Blair can't buy me off. But he's got to come with something serious.* And our problem as Black and Asian politicians is that all too often we allow ourselves to be sidelined and bought off all too easily instead of *hanging on for the greater prize.*

Education is crucial; in some ways, perhaps, the most crucial issue of all. And we want to be doing what we can do on Local Education Authorities to ensure that the needs of our children are being met. We want to be encouraging others in the community to go on these schools as Governors. Because now you know, Governors, they hire, they fire, they recruit. *In a way, it's more important at this time to encourage our people to be on school governing bodies than even to be Councillors.* And so we need to be taking an overview. We need to be taking a strategic overview and putting ourselves and putting our community where the power is – where the crucial issues are.

It's been fascinating to listen to our American colleague. I think one of the most important things that I have learnt from visits to America and the opportunity to meet with American politicians and when I have lectured at American Colleges and Universities, is that with all the problems, Black people in America, *politicians, the Church and business work much more closely together than they do here.* If we are going to achieve anything as Black and Asian politicians we have to understand that we need to be working very closely with our religious institutions and very closely with business people. Because for the Black and Asian community it is not either/or. It is not either you become a politician or you become involved in business.

We as Black and Asian people have to advance on all

> *...we allow ourselves to be sidelined and bought off all too easily instead of hanging on for the greater prize.*

fronts at once. And we will never be strong as Black and Asian politicians until our business people are strong.

Talking about mobilising the community, who is more able? Who is more effective at mobilising our communities than our religious institutions?

Who is more effective at mobilising our communities than our religious institutions?

So if there is one thing that we can learn from our brothers and sisters in the United States, it is how closely the Churches and business and politicians work together.

The other thing we can learn from them is the effectiveness of their *Affirmative Action* and Contracts Compliance Programme. It is Affirmative Action and Contracts Compliance which has set aside work for Black business people, which has done more to help Black business in the United States than many other things. Now as it stands, the Law in Britain wouldn't allow some of these things. But I will certainly be pressing, in my position on the National Executive of the Labour Party and as we come now to draw up our manifesto, for the Labour Party to commit itself to the type of Affirmative Action on Contracts Compliance Legislation which will enable Local Authorities to actually start channelling work to Black business and helping to build and support our Black and Asian business. I think that's crucial.

I have touched on the importance, I think, of locating yourself as a politician in the mainstream, rather than allowing yourself as a Black and Asian politician to be shuffled off the margin, saying that mainstream concerns are concerns to us.

I have touched on the importance of issues to do with economy, employment and business and the key importance of education. But you know the other thing that's very important for us as Black and Asian politicians and where we can learn from each other and learn from brothers and sisters in the United States, is how we conduct ourselves as individuals. Now you know I am going to say something which people might not like here but we cannot continue to allow ourselves on Local Authority after Local Authority to be used against each other.

Because you might think to yourself if I smile, smile, smile at this white committee chair I might get something for my community group and my street. But you see what they're playing is the game the British have played since the dawn of Empire: divide and rule. And you know because I'm a Member of Parliament in Westminster and obviously because of my concern for Black and Asian people, I hear and I see what's happening up and down the country. And what I see up and down the country is Local Authorities where the *Black and Asian Councillors could be more effective if they could only achieve a degree of unity.* Now I'm not saying that you must never fight and quarrel. All I'm saying is, for goodness sake, just try fighting and quarreling behind closed doors!! Because this is why – this is why to be blunt – this is why some of these cliques manage to run these Local Authorities year in year out: because we allow ourselves to be played off against each other. Whether it's played off against each other in terms of ethnic groups, or even played off

Black and Asian Councillors could be more effective if they could only achieve a degree of unity.

against each other in terms of individuals. And you may think in the short run, this week, this month, that you're the gainer but in the long run the entire Black and Asian community is the loser. And it is no good jumping up and cursing white people and demanding this and demanding that if we are not able to have a minimum level of unity.

In closing, let me say to you, when Keith and I were younger and perhaps a little more radical, when we were at the Labour Party Conference one year we stormed the platform. I think we were wearing our Black Section T-Shirts and I heard afterwards that one MP on the platform, who I won't name, turned to another MP – one of her colleagues – and said "What are these people doing in our Party?" Well, we have the answer here this morning – we are here to stay and here to fight and hopefully here to fight together, whether in our Local Authority, whether in the United States, we need a Black/Asian strategy, we need Black/Asian unity, a strategy and a unity that we have come too far to turn back from now.

Workshops

Workshop 1:
Racism in Local Democracy

Speakers:
Rajinder Sohpal, Reading Councillor
Presented Research Report into the experiences of Black,
Asian and Ethnic Minority Councillors, prepared
especially for the Convention.

Herman Ouseley, Chair Commission for Racial Equality

Main Issues

■ The need for a legally constituted national
organisation for Black and ethnic minority
councillors with regional networks.

■ The need for specialised training for newly elected
Councillors.

■ The need to improve communication between all
Black and Ethnic Minority Councillors.

Key Discussion Points

■ **The need for a legally constituted national**
organisation for Black and Asian Councillors.
Several examples were given of Black and Asian
Councillors who had been isolated by their
colleagues and were unable to progress their political

careers effectively. There was a strong feeling from the discussion of various Councillors that they were being marginalised in terms of mainstream political issues. Many Councillors felt a strong need to develop a national network of Black and Ethnic Minority Councillors to give focus, direction and national backing to local issues concerning Black people. There was a need to raise the profile of Black and Ethnic Minorities to create confidence and progress issues effectively. A majority of Councillors agreed that it was important to establish a national organisation across all parties.

All the Councillors expressed the view that such an organisation should establish serious and clear aims and not end up a 'talking shop' for Councillors. The organisation should be supported by all the major political parties with access to those political parties at both national and regional levels. It should also establish constructive working links with local authority associations (e.g. AMA, ADC, ALG), who should be encouraged to adopt a code of good conduct and develop a complaints procedure to deal with complaints of racist abuse and other problems of a racist nature between local politicians.

There was also a need to develop a code of ethics for Black Councillors towards each other. This was seen to be necessary as many Black and Asian Councillors were still comparatively inexperienced and have difficulty prioritising issues and reaching mutually advantageous decisions amicably and diplomatically.

■ *The need for training/information.*
The training programme should aim at confidence building as well as information and in depth knowledge of various areas of local authority working.

The results of the survey and research carried out by Councillor Rajinder Sohpal showed a very high turnover of Black and Asian Councillors. Approximately fifty percent were in their first term.

There was a clear expression of need for special training programmes for Black and Asian Councillors especially during the first two years.

■ *The need to improve information/communication between Black and Asian Councillors.*
There was discussion about the need the Black and Asian Councillors had to be able to access each other nationally and to be able to share views and develop joint working on various anti-racist policies.

Apart from a yearly convention of Black and Asian Councillors it would also be useful to have ongoing dialogue.

There should be an annual programme of 'brain storming' development of joint strategies, seminars, training, where communication would greatly enhance the confidence and operation of Black and Asian Councillors.

The workshop members were particularly concerned about the lack of briefing and quality information given by senior officers to Black and

Asian Councillors. The collusion of officers and non-Black Councillors often resulted in the blocking of positive progress on equalities issues.

There also needs to be strong awareness training to allow Councillors to develop strategies on the "divide and rule" phenomena in local authorities, and to be able to contribute constructively to the anti-racist cause.

Recommendations

■ A legally constituted National Organisation of Black and Ethnic Minority Councillors to be established.

■ A full developmental training programme for Councillors to address special areas in connection with anti-racist working, etc.

■ A programme of seminars, conferences and smaller 'brain-storming' meetings should be organised at regular intervals.

Workshop 2:
Racial Harassment

Speakers:
Joe Allen, Leicester City Councillor
Mehboob Ladha, Leicester's Race Relations Officer

Main Issues

■ The need for legislative change in terms of racial harassment.

■ The need for local authorities to be seen to be taking action to tackle racial harassment (e.g. evictions).

Key Discussion Points

■ *The need for stronger legislation.* It has been estimated that 140,000 incidents of racial attacks and harassment occur every year in Britain; that is 380 attacks daily. Yet in Leicester, for example, the City Council has managed to secure only 3 evictions and served 7 notices seeking possessions amongst tenants who have been identified as perpetrators in the last two years. The lack of an effective legislative strategy was seen as a major barrier. The Crown Prosecution Service was criticised for not taking the issue seriously either by dropping cases because of lack of evidence or by failing to prosecute effectively in court. The police were also criticised for not working in tandem with local authorities and for not dealing with racism amongst its own ranks.

Also, very often the victims find themselves in court rather than the alleged perpetrators. The Convention should call for stronger measures from the Government to combat the activities of far-right extremist groups who are responsible for organised racial harassment incidents.

- *The need for more effective local authority action.* Councils need to use existing powers more effectively when combating racial harassment. Monitoring systems should be established to ascertain the progress of racial harassment cases and where barriers occur. Councillors should ensure anti-racial harassment policies are adhered to by officers. There should be a co-ordinated system of training for all officers in a local authority. A network should be established to discover the real extent of the problem and also share good practice; for example, some areas have set up multi-agency forums and could help neighbouring authorities.

Recommendations

- The proposed Association for Black Councillors should take the lead in fighting racial harassment.

- There should be a co-ordinated approach to racial harassment, with existing multi-agency forums sharing good practice.

- All local authorities should develop an effective training and awareness programme for both members and officers.

- The Convention should lobby MPs to enhance and strengthen the legal framework.

- There should be more support to develop community action/participation in dealing with racial harassment.

- There should be resources to develop a national database for reporting active cases of racial harassment.

Workshop 3:
Black Women in Politics

Speakers:
Neelam Bakshi, Strathclyde Regional Councillor
Jagir Sekhon, L.B. Greenwich Councillor

Main Issues

- To explore the experience of Black women in politics and identify the barriers to genuine participation and representation.

- To propose solutions and strategies for overcoming these barriers.

Key Discussion Points

- **Barriers.** Despite having women-only shortlists for Parliamentary candidates, the Labour Party have yet to nominate a Black woman. Although this is important in itself, there are still barriers in trades unions, school governing bodies and with appointments to quangos such as hospital trusts. Firstly, there seem to be barriers that all women face, e.g. lack of creche facilities at council meetings held in the evenings. Secondly, Black women also face barriers amongst some white colleagues who may be supportive of tackling sexism but have a colour-blind approach to confronting racism. Many women have to support a family and have little or no remuneration for their work as a Councillor.

Recommendations

- Black women need to establish their own national forum and within the proposed Association for Black Councillors.

- Black women need to be represented on selection boards and interview panels for appointments.

- Black women are marginalised onto Race or Equalities Committees; they need to participate on mainstream committees such as housing and education.

- Black women need to have the means to network and support each other, Councillors as well as officers.

Workshop 4:
Economic Development

Chair:
Mee Ling Ng, Lewisham Councillor

Speakers:
Mohammed Ajeeb, Bradford Councillor
Atiha Mohamed, Assistant Director of Centre for Local Economic Strategies

Main Issues

■ In general, urban regeneration is not just about spatial developments and infrastructural improvements. This top down approach does not take into consideration the human aspects of development.

■ The current Government policy failed on urban regeneration through its usage of development corporations, especially London Dockland Development Corporation (LDDC). This policy has had particular impact on inner city areas where the majority of Black communities live and they have suffered very much at the hands of these policies.

■ Urban policies do have an impact on rural communities particularly with new town developments in rural areas.

■ Inner cities have been neglected for many years particularly with very large scale inhuman public housing developments, structures that lack community facilities and spirit. These have left councils with a legacy of things to be put right.

- The economic recession particularly devastated Black communities and especially the unemployed, long term unemployed people, disenfranchised young people and families on low income.

- As a large proportion of Black communities are urbanised, the need to look at policies and practical initiatives to actually meet the needs of the communities falls on Councillors who are themselves originally from these communities.

- The skills of Black and Asian communities who arrived in Britain during the '50s and '60s actually became suddenly obsolete to them. This is one of the reasons why unemployment among these communities is much higher than the indigenous population. The unemployed members of these communities need to be retrained in areas where there are skill shortages.

- The mass unemployment of Black and ethnic minority youth is also an issue. New skills should be gained by considering new opportunities.

- Growing unemployment pushed Black and Ethnic Minority communities to start their own businesses. Most of them are located in the service sector, serving the daily needs of local communities. Many of them opened corner grocer shops. However, to continue and survive is now becoming more difficult as they face the problem of competition from the growing number of superstores.

■ The Black and ethnic minority high street retail shops, textiles, restaurants and other businesses do attract trade from tourists from other cities and Europe.

■ A number of councils recently are assisting with a development of the restaurant trade, small business initiatives, shop front improvements, the building and improvement of business premises, providing training in good food preparation, and hygiene courses.

■ Local businesses also work in close co-operation with the local Training and Enterprise Council, housing, environment and health departments of the councils or city councils.

■ Recession is not confined to one country or Europe, it is world-wide and swift global changes have led to uncertainty in every aspect of life.

Recommendations

■ The way forward is to develop an urban policy which should:

- articulate a strategic vision

- involve real community empowerment

- be based on partnership. The concept of partnership needs to be articulated by considering questions such as what do we mean by real partnership, what kind of balances there are between partners.

- Social issues such as deprivation, racism, crime, poverty are an integral part of the economic issues therefore they should be solved by a more co-ordinated approach.

- The policies should also integrate the environmental issues such as pollution, health, traffic and so on.

- There have been lots of technological changes over the years to which urban policies have to respond.

- Currently job markets offer different types of work matching skills. Training needs to be developed.

- The needs of diverse workforces should be looked at. There are more women in the labour market. Childcare and all other related issues need to be taken into consideration.

- Urban policy makers should use expert organisations such as the CLES to develop strategies.

- Mass unemployment of Black communities in certain areas should be viewed by considering the following points:

  - racism and discrimination

  - race equality

  - poverty

  - poor housing

  - lack of access to training, jobs, information

  - low pay

  - poor working conditions

- health

- concentration in declining sectors (e.g. manufacturing industries). Some other sectors which are developing very fast are technologically far more advanced than these declining sectors.

■ Single Regeneration Budget (SRB) is not going to be effective to Black communities. Local boroughs should organise a nationwide very well run campaign to keep Section 11 type of special grants.

■ Black and ethnic minority business sectors must be given maximum help through carefully planned innovative projects to increase their dynamism and get into the sectors where the future lies.

■ Urban policy reports need to develop sections on the special needs of Black and ethnic minority communities.

■ Black and ethnic minority communities need to recognise the importance of new technology. Councils should ensure that they help Black and ethnic minority communities to adopt and understand the changing employment patterns and show the reason behind the higher unemployment of Black people.

■ Most of the local economic development approaches are colour blind. The need to develop strong support to Black and ethnic minority communities and mainstream their needs is paramount.

■ Local Black and ethnic minority communities should acquire the necessary information and skills to get into sub-contracting. CCT and other contracts should go to the Black community. Councils need to encourage these communities.

■ A proper strategy and action programme needs to be built to preserve the environment by developing an argument against consumerism.

■ Black Councillors must not give the impression to white colleagues that they are only there for Black people.

Workshop 5: Equal Opportunities in Employment

Chair:
Muhammed Afzal, Birmingham City Councillor

Speakers:
Ramani Chelliah, Local Government Information Unit
Henry Coore, Birmingham City Council
Mahtab Khan, Birmingham City Council

Main Issues

■ The role of local authorities in a changing political environment.

■ Identify strategies to overcome obstacles and challenges faced in promoting best practice.

Key Discussion Points

■ Need to recognise the link between different equal opportunities policies (e.g. Race and Gender).

■ Policies have to be adapted in the light of changing circumstances (e.g. introduction of Community Care Legislation, Local Management of Schools) which has meant that the council has become an enabler rather than a provider of services.

■ Councils must adopt workforce monitoring to ensure any contractions in employment do not impact adversely on Black staff.

- Positive action should be used more often (e.g. Section 71 of the Race Relations Act) allowing for Black staff to be recruited for particular posts.

- Councils also have a duty to ensure firms which tender for contracted out services are asked specific questions on race equality.

Recommendations

- Positive action initiatives are essential. These include management development programmes and the use of secondments.

- Councils should invest in 'employee care' initiatives. While many local authorities are being forced to reduce workforces, and are not recruiting, the staff that are left should remain motivated. In this respect, equal opportunities policies should recognise cultural or religious diversity and deal with racial or sexual harassment.

- Monitoring should encompass not only the recruitment of staff but also include matters relating to retention. For example, any workforce analysis should be able to identify the progress of Black staff within the council.

- Above all there should be political will and the community must be able to see how the targets are being met (e.g. the idea of a Chief Officer's Annual Report was raised).

Workshop 6:
Race Equality Standard

Chair:
Nirmal Roy, Camden Councillor

Speaker:
Ronnie Wilson, Commission for Racial Equality

Main Issues

■ To present an overview of the CRE's Standard for Race Equality in Local Government.

■ To enable attenders of the workshop to implement the Standard in their own local authority.

Key Discussion Points

■ The Standard came out of the 'Effectiveness Review' undertaken by the CRE of 42 local authorities. Most of these had equal opportunities policies but under half have full and comprehensive ethnic monitoring.

■ The CRE Standard is intended to bring Race Equality into the mainstream by providing simple, clear and practical advice. By using the Standard local authorities can measure progress in five areas:

● policy and planning

● service delivery and Customer Care

● community development

- employment   (Recruitment and Selection)
  (Developing and Retaining Staff)

- marketing and corporate image

■ In each of the five areas progress is measured from a minimum level (1) to an optimum level (5). At each of the five levels there are a desired set of outcomes.

■ Some members of the workshop felt that as the Standard was only advice and not legislation, there was a need for Councillors to be responsible for ensuring officers implement it. In doing this there is a need for comprehensive ethnic monitoring. Councils need to ensure equalities is not marginalised and that Race Equality has a high profile both corporately and within each department.

Recommendations

■ The Standard needs to be disseminated to all relevant staff.

■ The CRE should establish a national database of Black Councillors, with information on their particular interests. This could also be used to gain more knowledge of council structures.

■ Chief Officers need to be assessed in relation to achievement of race equality targets.

■ The Standard needs to include services subject to CCT.

■ In setting Standards, councils should empower community groups and enable their active participation in local authority service provision.

Workshop 7:
New Ways of Meeting
Community Needs

Chair:
Lester Holloway, Hammersmith and Fulham Councillor

Speakers:
Nazir Ahmed, Rotherham Council
Nitin Thakrar, British Trust for Conservation Volunteers

Main Issues

■ Identify methods and systems for identifying gaps in service provision to ethnic minorities.

■ Review the support given to the Black voluntary sector.

Key Discussion Points

■ Local Authorities need to formally establish consultative mechanisms with Black and ethnic minority communities. Where do these report to? Do they have automatic rights to place items on committee agendas?

■ Local community groups need to link in with other local and national Black voluntary sector groups.

■ How inclusive are Black organisations? Do they involve young people and women?

■ Community development initiatives need to tie into anti-poverty measures.

- Councillors play a pivotal role and can bring relevant officers and community groups together.

Recommendations

- A Directory of Black, Asian and ethnic minority Councillors should be published.

- There should be regular bulletins produced targeted at Black councillors.

- Councillors should be more pro-active in holding surgeries in places where Black communities meet e.g. religious centres.

- The proposed Association of Black Councillors should compile a register of community development initiatives so that good practice can be shared.

Workshop 8:
Local Authorities Against Racism in Europe

Chair:
Narendra Makanji, L.B. Haringey Councillor

Speakers:
Kingsley Abrams, L.B. Merton Councillor
Talal Karim, L.B. Islington Councillor

Main Issues

■ The importance of the EU in combating racism.

■ The continued rise of racism in EU countries.

■ The need to form a Local Authorities Against Racism network

Key Discussion Points

■ ***The role of the European Union.*** The 1996 Inter-Governmental Conference will hear agreement for a European Directive on race equality in employment and service provision. Yet this same conference will also hear Britain's proposals to retain border controls and thus mitigate against a free movement of people within the EU. The EU also requires visas from 127 countries, most of which are in the Southern hemisphere. Within the EU itself Black and ethnic minority people encounter difficulties regarding their residence status. Furthermore, EU countries are restricting the rights of refugees seeking asylum.

■ *Local Authorities Against Racism.* The Association of London Authorities (ALA) had sponsored a conference on racism whose purpose was to co-ordinate local authority action and link with partners in Europe. A Declaration Against Racism was signed by all participants. The issue of networking is of prime importance. We need to learn from the experience of Local Authorities Against Apartheid, which has worked well in the last decade.

Recommendations

■ That this convention should be a fore-runner of an annual Convention of Black Councillors and that a steering committee be elected as soon as possible to organise this and related efforts.

■ That all local authorities should adopt the Declaration Against Racism (overleaf) and network with local authorities across Britain and Europe.

■ That the convention writes to the Secretary of State to seek Black representation on the committee for the Regions and to pursue an agreed lobbying strategy to achieve racial equality in Europe in particular on the issue of free movements/open borders and recognition of overseas qualifications.

■ That the convention establish a series of research and information exchange processes such as a directory – who's who of Black Councillors.

Local Authorities Against Racism

London, 26 February 1994

We, the undersigned, express our joint concern about the rise of racism and xenophobia within Europe.

We pledge not to tolerate racism, xenophobia, racial discrimination or racial harassment within our community, that we shall do all within our power to eliminate racial discrimination, racism and xenophobia, to promote equality of opportunity and good relations between all of our residents.

This declaration forms the basis of an initiative linking local government across Britain and Europe in a co-ordinated effort to address the current rise of racism and xenophobia.

In signing the declaration local authorities commit themselves to enacting its underlying principles by:

- Exposing and condemning the incidence of racism and xenophobia in our communities;

- Mobilising the resources of our local councils and communities to develop and promote local strategies to combat racism;

- Linking our local activity to the wider national and European anti-racist networks.

They Said That...

Nearly 300 Councillors attended the conference and many contributed during the plenary sessions. There were also a number of 'VIPs' who were unable to attend. Here's a selection of what they said ...

From the Prime Minister's Office

'The Prime Minister has asked me to thank you for your letter dated the 13th October inviting him to attend the National Convention for Asian, African Caribbean and Ethnic Minority Councillors on the 31st March. Sadly the Prime Minister's existing diary commitments that afternoon make it impossible for him to join you and he must decline your kind invitation. He is sorry to send you a disappointing reply but sends you and all concerned his very best wishes for a successful and enjoyable occasion.'

Tony Blair - the Leader of the Opposition

'I send you my warm wishes for the success of the Black, Asian and Ethnic Minorities Convention. This is a historic development and I hope that it will be a very successful occasion. I hope to come to some future occasion.'

Paddy Ashdown - the Leader of the Liberal Democrat Party

'I am writing to send you my good wishes for the success of the Convention. I cannot be present, but I know that Simon Hughes will be joining you this evening at the House of Commons.'

Bill Morris - the General Secretary of the Transport and General Workers' Union

'I acknowledge with thanks receipt of your letter of the 13th October. I very much regret that I shall be unable to accept your kind invitation as I am due to lead a TUC Delegation on a visit to South Africa at that time. My very best wishes to all concerned for a successful Conference.'

The South African High Commissioner

'Thank you for your letter of the 23rd February concerning the National Convention for Black, Asian and Ethnic Minority Councillors. As you would be aware the cornerstone of South Africa's present policies is non-racialism and I therefore wish you all success in your deliberations.'

Councillor Mirza - Birmingham City Council

'I want to mention that because the Conservative Party is the ruling party, this does not mean to say that we do not represent the Black and Asian communities - we do. The issue is that we in Britain should be liberal minded and that colour should not be a barrier. Being coloured and in the Conservative Party, I do not feel segregated in any way and that is why I want to encourage others to join other parties and have the patience to listen to others.'

Councillor Bakshi - Strathcylde Regional Council

'I was very sad to see that our intolerance and bigotry did not allow a person of different ideology to spell out his views. He happened to be Tory, I am a practicing Socialist.'

Councillor Mee Ling Ng - Lewisham Council

'There are very few Black women Councillors and so the Black Sisters are very thin on the ground. I have been a Councillor for 9 years and I hope some of the workshops this afternoon, not just the Women's workshops, can actually address the mechanisms and structures, which can actually help Black women to get on to the political ladder.'

Councillor Spence - Birmingham City Council

'When we come to Conventions like this, members will talk and talk sweetly and nicely because words are cheap. The important thing is when we leave this Convention, we go away and do what we said we would do. It is no good coming up year after year and saying the same things over again. We need to stand up, take stock and look.'

Councillor Jones - Buckinghamshire County Council

'Yes they have got Black people in Buckinghamshire. There are 71 County Councillors and one Black Ethnic Minority Councillor. I am he.'

Councillor Baker - Southampton City Council

'There is a time to work with people to politicise them and to get them involved in the process. The Government is actually hitting Black people with its

current policies on pay more than anyone else. We
need to realise that we are not politicians if we ignore
the streets which we supposedly came from.'

Herman Ouseley - Commission for Racial Equality

'From today you have got to be above the petty
politics, you have got to be above the factionalism, you
have got to be above just concentrating on the small
prize, because the bigger prize is a better Britain. We
have got to be here, only 6 out of every 100 are us, we
do not overrun Britain, and we do not hold the levers
of power, but collectively and wisely and systematically
and astutely we can achieve a hell of a lot.'

Keith Vaz - Member of Parliament

'This is for me a dream come true. I could not believe
that we could all do this and it has been tremendously
successful. Not a single row; even SWISS TV have left
saying they cannot believe it has been so well organised
and everyone so friendly to each other. I hope, when
the Steering Committee meets, they decide to take this
forward. The key thing is do not fight; work together
and I think you can build together a very powerful
organisation.'

The Way Forward

Cllr Mee Ling Ng

There is tremendous support for a national caucus of Black, Asian and ethnic minority Councillors to be set up in this country. This was strongly echoed in the contributions from the floor and in most of the workshops. Not only were delegates inspired by Congressman Frazer but Councillors recognised the need for a national association which can provide leadership and direction in local government for race equality and a better deal for the communities we represent.

Black, Asian and ethnic minority Councillors together, can be a force with the power to influence the agenda at both local and central government levels. Once established, the national association can champion the interests of Black and ethnic minority people in all issues that affect them economically, socially and politically. A commitment to an all-party association can only strengthen the community's voice as will total unity between Black, Asian and ethnic minority Councillors on key issues affecting our communities. This unity in common purpose was achieved at the Convention and should be the hallmark of the national association.

The value of networking cannot be overstated. Some Councillors are isolated simply because of their numbers whilst others are marginalised from power within their authorities. Many have achieved despite the odds and some hold key positions within local government. Never before has there been an opportunity for Councillors to come together, to share our experiences and to find strength, support and renewed determination to achieve our personal objectives and to make a real difference to the opportunities and resources afforded to our communities. Now is the time to build on the achievements and work actively to encourage and support more Black, Asian and ethnic minority people to participate fully in the democratic process.

In the wider context of the European Union, Britain is seen to have progressive legislation on race equality. We know what lies between the reality and the rhetoric. It is therefore crucial to articulate our experiences, at both local and national levels, in order to influence the debates on a whole range of issues such as immigration policies, economic policies and social policies. Diane Abbott MP called for colleagues to get involved in the mainstream of decision making: the challenge is in maintaining the pressure for equality whilst ensuring that the mainstream agenda is inclusive of the needs, interests and aspirations of all our peoples.

Without a doubt there is a race equality agenda to take forward into the next millennium.

There is no shortage of work to be done. There are pressing issues like racism and racial harassment to tackle, improving employment opportunities in local government, pursuing contract compliance, building partnerships with voluntary organisations, black businesses and religious organisations, to increase participation of colleagues and local Black and ethnic minority people in the democratic institutions of this country and not least of all build alliances and galvanise the forces to achieve a better and more just society.

Without a doubt there is a race equality agenda to take forward into the next millennium. We must seize the time and organise to make gains for our communities. It is a long road ahead for us and the next step must be to build the national association which will be the vehicle to help us on our journey.

Survey of Councillors

Cllr Rajinder Sohpal and Claire Muir

Introduction

Many Black councillors have suggested that two very powerful influences have a serious impact on their work and their political progress.

The first is that their "constituency" goes well beyond the electoral boundaries because they are seen as a source of strength for issues affecting Black and ethnic minority communities generally. Indeed, their peers in the council may reinforce this influence.

The second is that Black councillors receive a different and detrimental treatment by the political machinery.

A fundamental aim of this survey has been to provide a completely "risk-free" platform for some honest views about some of the important issues affecting Black politicians and their aspirations.

The response rate has been fantastic and the information collected is extremely valuable. The report is an important resource for councils, political parties, local authority associations and others interested in local democracy. It is a valuable tool to enable a rational discussion of some sensitive and important issues without expecting individual Black politicians to "expose" themselves.

The survey and the findings have been motivated by one major concern, that is, to increase the confidence and participation rates, of the Black communities, in local democracy.

It would be foolish and unproductive to evade the findings of this survey with excuses of how it could have been done better. It is hoped that instead, everyone will put their minds and energies to implementing the recommendations and other constructive ideas.

Background

In preparation for the First National Black, Asian and Ethnic Minority Councillors Convention on 31st March 1995 a survey of Black councillors was undertaken. The survey was the first of its kind in Britain and aimed to identify Black councillors' experiences and perceptions of the local democratic system. The survey looked at the demographic pattern of Black councillors in Britain; opportunities for Black councillors to hold leadership positions in local government; their experience of racism from other councillors and council officials; their feelings about the current action being taken by local government to address equal opportunity issues and the views of Black women councillors compared to their male counterparts.

Methodology

The exact number of Black councillors nationally is not known. No formal records appear to be kept of the ethnic breakdown of individual local authorities. It is thought that there are around 600 Black councillors nationally. The London Borough of Hounslow recently undertook a survey of the numbers of Black councillors nationally and had the names of 419 Black councillors returned to them. These 419 councillors were used for this survey. Each councillor was sent a questionnaire and asked to complete and return it. 168 councillors responded. This was a response rate of 40% which is extremely good for a postal questionnaire. The good response may well reflect the concern that Black councillors had for getting their opinions recorded but it may also be to do with the fact that respondents were

Figure 1: Ethnic Group of Respondents

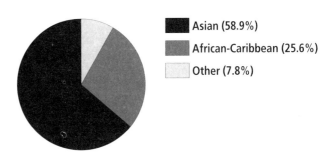

Asian (58.9%)

African-Caribbean (25.6%)

Other (7.8%)

given complete assurance that their responses would be confidential. It is strongly recommended that councils and local authority associations urgently collate a comprehensive ethnic profile of their councillors and provide the statistical data to the Black councillors' network.

Findings of the Survey

Demographic pattern of Black Councillors

Of the 168 respondents:

Gender

141 (84%) were male

27 (16%) were female

The number of female respondents was very small, indicating a low representation of women amongst Black councillors. The small sample makes it difficult to draw any real conclusions as to the representativeness of the female respondents. That needs to be remembered throughout the report.

Ethnic Group

58.9%   described themselves as Asian

25.6%   described themselves as Afro-Caribbean★

7.8%   represented a range of other ethnic groups

(See figure 1)

Length of Time as a Councillor

45% of the respondents had been councillors for less than four years. While some (12.7%) of the male respondents had been councillors for over 12 years none of the female respondents had been councillors for more than 12 years.

The predominance of short terms of office may either be an indication of high turnover of Black councillors through disillusionment or that more Black people have taken political office over the last four years

★ *Apologies are made for an error in the wording of the questionnaire. A number of respondents made the comment that "Afro-Carribbean" is not a category and "African-Caribbean" is the correct term.*

Figure 2: Number of years a councillor (by gender)

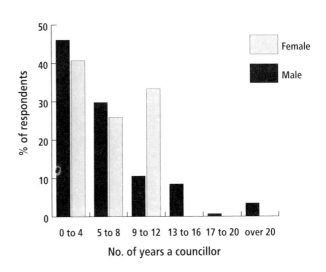

than previously. In any case, councils and political parties must give urgent consideration to a post election care and support package (figure 2). See also section on 'Satisfaction with Race Policy' (page 83)

Type of Authority

57.1 % of the respondents were Borough councillors. None of the respondents were Parish councillors. (See graph 3).

The lack of Black councillors in Parish councils is probably a result of the Black communities tending to be in urban rather than the rural areas represented by Parish councils.

Opportunities for Leadership

19.1%   of the respondents had been committee chairs

22%   of the respondents had been major sub-committee chairs

48.8% of the respondents had been working party chairs

6.5% of the respondents had been party leader

3% of the respondents had been deputy party leader

13.7% of the respondents had been mayor

18.2% of Asian respondents and 16.3% of African-Caribbean respondents had been committee chairs.

27.9% of African-Caribbean respondents and 10.1% of Asian respondents had been mayor.

The rate or likelihood of chairing main or major sub-committees is difficult to assess without comparison with white colleagues. However, the interesting thing seems to be the high incidence of Black mayors. This could be seen to be suggesting one or both of the following:

i) a positive use of role modelling of Black politicians;

ii) the award of "Putty Medals" for calm because mayors have no power. If this were the case then African and Caribbean councillors seem to be getting side-lined more frequently than Asian councillors.

Councils should consider seriously the use of the roles of mainstream committee chairs as the method for promoting role models. In particular, African Caribbean councillors need to be better supported for such positions.

Satisfaction with Opportunities for Prominent Roles

Respondents were asked how satisfied they were with the opportunities that were available to them for prominent roles within the council.

The majority were satisfied (61.9%). There were lower satisfaction levels amongst the African-Caribbean respondents (51.2% satisfied while 69.7% of Asian respondents were satisfied). There were distinct differences between the satisfaction levels of male and female respondents. The highest ranking satisfaction level for male respondents was "fairly satisfied" at 52.3% but for the female respondents it was "very dissatisfied" at 33.3%. This indicates that Black women councillors' opportunities for prominent roles are being disadvantaged by their sex in addition to any disadvantage they may experience on racial grounds.

Although the majority of respondents said they were satisfied with their opportunities for prominent roles, a significant 35% were dissatified with their opportunities. This suggests a high level of discontent which may well cause the high levels of turnover referred to in *'Length of Time as a Councillor'* above.

Figure 3: Type of Authority

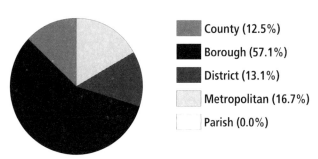

County (12.5%)
Borough (57.1%)
District (13.1%)
Metropolitan (16.7%)
Parish (0.0%)

How Colleagues See Respondents

Respondents were asked whether they felt their colleagues saw them as a councillor representing predominantly "mainstream"/general issues or ethnic minority issues or women's issues.

The majority (66.7%) felt they were predominantly seen as "mainstream" councillors. 26.2% felt they were predominantly seen as representing ethnic minority issues. Of the female respondents 11.1% felt they were predominantly seen as representing women's issues.

If one in four Black councillors is seen as representing mainly ethnic minority issues, then there is a strong likelihood that many will be chairs of working groups or sub-committees concerning such issues. The same stereotypes will reduce the likelihood of other mainstream leading roles. The results of the survey show that housing (5.4%), equalities (4.2%), social services (3.6%) and leisure (3%) are the highest ranking main committees chaired by respondents. Those who do become chairs appear to have been responsible for mainstream committees. But the numbers of Black councillors getting chairs of committees and sub-committees is so low that there appears to be a problem with Black councillors getting mainstream chairs at all. The 48% chairing working groups seems to bear this out.

Councils should seriously consider enabling black councillors to move into the mainstream.

The figures indicate that in addition to a quarter of the Black female respondents feeling that they are seen predominantly as representing ethnic minority interests, another 11% feel they are seen as representing predominantly women's interests. So it appears that Black women councillors are doubly marginalised.

Political Aspirations

Respondents were asked if they felt that their political aspirations had been affected on racial grounds negatively, positively, not at all.

34.5%   felt there had been no effect.

19%   felt that there had been a negative effect.

39.9%   felt that there had been a positive effect.

They were also asked if they felt that their political aspirations had been affected on gender grounds negatively, positively, not at all.

The response of the female councillors was fairly evenly spread across all three (29.6% of the women felt there was a positive affect) while the majority of male respondents (68.8%) tended to feel that there was no effect.

A third of the respondents feeling that they were racially discriminated against represents a very significant size of discontent. This is a very serious issue. It is recommended that the local authority associations sponsor some further work by the Black councillors' network to get a more detailed picture of the causes and a clear strategy for what solutions councils can consider adopting.

On a more positive note, it seems that significant numbers of Black councillors feel that their racial origin has assisted them in the process. Almost a third of female respondents also felt that the fact that they were a women had helped them. However, the small sample size of the female respondents must be remembered.

Support from Political Party

Respondents were asked if they felt the support of their party had been affected on racial grounds.

48.8%   felt there had been no effect.

29.2%   felt that there had been a negative effect.

13.1%   felt that there had been a positive effect.

They were also asked if they felt the support of their party had been affected on gender grounds. The majority of both sexes felt there had been no effect. 18.5% of the women felt that there had been a positive effect.

However, a suggestion from almost one third of the respondents that their political party had discriminated against them could signal much higher discontent in the community generally. This assertion is based on the belief that those who have managed to get elected as councillors ought to have more confidence in their party than others who may not have succeeded or even tried. Confidence building measures should be considered by the main political parties.

Experience of Racist Comments/Behaviour

Respondents were asked whether they had ever received racist comments/behaviour from other councillors or council officers. (See figure 4).

Figure 4: Respondents who have received racist comments or behaviour

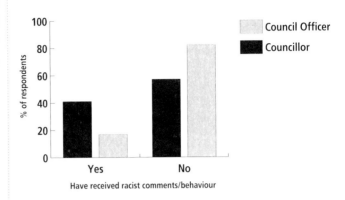

From Other Councillors

57.1%   of respondents had never received racist comments/behaviour from other councillors.

41.1%   of respondents had received racist comments/behaviour from other councillors.

12.5%   had received at least one racist comment/behaviour from another councillor in the last month.

The rate of racist abuse from colleagues is disturbingly high. Dismissing this as "harmless jokes" or "over-sensitivity" is sometimes a way in which such behaviour is tolerated. This is clearly not acceptable. The standard of behaviour of councillors towards each other should improve to the levels that many council policies expect from their officers and service users.

The local authority associations should urgently consider adopting a code of good behaviour/conduct, along with a sensitive complaints procedure.

From Council Officers

82.1% of respondents had never received racist comments/behaviour from council officers.

16.7% of respondents had received racist comments/behaviour from council officers.

3.6% had received at least one racist comment/behaviour from a council officer in the last month.

Behaviour from paid officers which can be deemed to be insulting or abusive would normally be dealt with as misconduct or gross misconduct. However, it seems that racist behaviour is not regarded as a disciplinary offence in that many councils. This is bad for any system of authority and must contribute to ways in which Black councillors become marginalised. Every chief executive should urgently review the position in their own council and make it very clear that abuse of any sort cannot be tolerated and that racist behaviour is regarded as gross misconduct. If necessary, internal disciplinary procedures must be revamped.

From the comments received in the survey there is a problem of officers who fail to support Black councillors in the way that they do white councillors. The Black councillors' network could usefully do some more work on the issue in the future.

Experience of Sexist Comments/Behaviour

Respondents were also asked whether they had ever received sexist comments/behaviour from other councillors or council officers. This was asked of both sexes.

From Other Councillors

48.1%   of the female respondents had received sexist comments/behaviour from other councillors compared to 10.6% of the male respondents.

14.8%   of the women had received at least one sexist comment/behaviour from another councillor in the last month.

Sexist behaviour from councillors is again cause for concern. Councils and local authority associations need to act to improve the code of conduct in relation to this.

From Council Officers

11.1%   of the female respondents had received sexist comments/behaviour from council officers compared to 4.9% of the male respondents.

Whilst incidence of sexist behaviour from officers is lower, it is still significant and indicates the low respect some officers give to female and Black members.

Figure 5: Networking

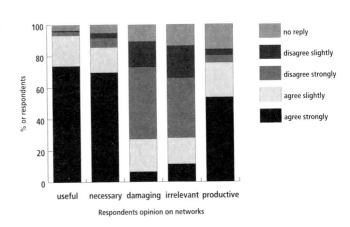

Disciplinary procedures should be amended to ensure that sexist behaviour is seen as gross misconduct.

Networking on Racial Equality Matters

Respondents were asked if they regularly liaised with other African-Caribbean, Asian or ethnic minority councillors about racial equality matters.

64.9% of respondents did liaise regularly with other "Black" councillors, 25% were involved in formal networks.

Networking on Gender Equality Matters

The female respondents were asked the same question regarding liaison with other women councillors on gender equality issues.

Almost half of them did liaise regularly but only four were involved in formal networks.

Opinion on Networks

Respondents were asked to indicate whether or not they agreed with the following phrases:

Networks are:

a) useful for sharing information,

b) necessary to enable ethnic minority groups to organise themselves,

c) damaging because they marginalise equalities issues,

d) irrelevant because equalities issues can be dealt with elsewhere,

e) productive because new schemes can be pioneered

through them.

Figure 5 shows the overwhelming support respondents gave to networks in their answers to the question.

The survey indicates a large degree of co-operation between Black councillors on race related issues and women councillors on gender issues. This is good news. We are ready to move on to a more formal and systematic process of networking.

Local authority associations should formally endorse support from a framework of national and regional networking. Practical and financial support should be allocated. Local councils should enable active participation of their Black councillors and formally approve attendance at such meetings. Members services could be enhanced to make available support to those councillors who wish to take a leading role.

Black women councillors should be actively encouraged to participate in national/regional networks for women members.

The results also help to show that the vast majority

Figure 6: Satisfaction with Race Policy

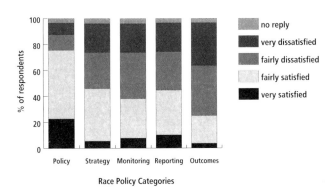

F A C I N G   T H E   C H A L L E N G E

of Black councillors do not agree with a notion sometimes stated (almost always by white politicians of all political persuasions) that Black networking is damaging. Such criticism is often put in the form of "segregation..." or "we should be seen as socialist, conservative.....first".

Satisfaction with Race Policy

Respondents were asked how satisfied they were with the following aspects of their council's equal opportunity policy on race:

a) the policy itself,

b) the strategy for implementation,

c) the monitoring process,

d) the process for reporting to members,

e) seeing real outcomes.

The majority of respondents (75.6%) were satisfied with the policy itself. However satisfaction levels went down considerably regarding the other aspects. More than half the respondents were dissatisfied with the other aspects of their council's race policy. Dissatisfaction was up to 71.4% on "Seeing real outcomes". (See figure 6.)

There are no real surprises here. Policy statements are easy to draw up. Some are even accompanied by record keeping and monitoring. However, very few are seen to actually deliver the goods. Yet, one could easily get the impression from white politicians that things are progressing well.

The way in which large amounts of resources are deployed apparently without much success, must be seriously questioned at the political level. At the same time, those councils who have injected little resources or action must make it a priority to work towards fair-play.

Satisfaction with Gender Policy

Respondents were asked the same question regarding their council's equal opportunity policy on gender.

Male respondents were consistently more satisfied with all aspects of the Gender Policy than the female respondents. 51.8% of the female respondents were satisfied with the policy itself but were progressively more dissatisfied with all the other aspects of the policy. 62.9% of them were dissatisfied with "Seeing real outcomes". 42.5% of the male respondents also indicated their dissatisfaction with this aspect.

The high dissatisfaction levels amongst both sexes on the outcomes of gender equality policy suggests a higher degree of shared perspective than we are often led to believe.

Promotion of Employment and Advancement on a Fair and Equitable Basis

Respondents were asked how satisfied they were that their council was taking all possible action to promote employment and advancement on a fair and equitable basis. There was an almost equal split between those who were satisfied and those who were dissatisfied.

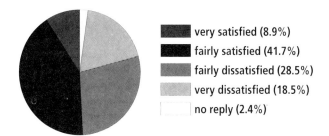

very satisfied (8.9%)
fairly satisfied (41.7%)
fairly dissatisfied (28.5%)
very dissatisfied (18.5%)
no reply (2.4%)

Figure 7: Satisfaction with Quality of Service to Ethnic Minority Communities

Provision of Quality Services

The same question was asked on the provision of relevant and good quality services to ethnic minority communities.

Again there was an almost even split between those who were satisfied and those who were dissatisfied. (See figure 7).

For reasons given in the introduction, most Black councillors would be under pressure to take an active interest in the service provision for Black communities across their council. The fact that only half feel satisfied with the achievements is very significant. It seems to indicate that the influence of Black councillors on service provision is limited. The solution to the problem lies, in part, with a strong networking system for Black councillors so that ideas can be shared and developed for how to bring about improvements. Another way will be for black councillors to get those opportunities to direct policy on services by being chairs of service committees which they are currently not doing in great numbers.

Acknowledgements and Thanks

The credit for the convention idea must go to Keith Vaz MP, Hounslow Council's deputy leader Cllr Jagdish Sharma MBE was inspired to host the convention and council officers, Robert Kerslake (Chief Executive) and Munira Thobani (Head of Equalities) helped turn the vision into the historic event that was the first Convention of Black, Asian and Ethnic Minority Councillors.

The Steering Group of Councillors was as follows: Councillor Rajinder Sohpal from Reading, Councillor Muhammed Afzal from Birmingham, Councillor Mee Ling Ng from Lewisham, Councillor Joe Allen from Leicester, Councillor Lester Holloway from Hammersmith and Fulham, Councillor Narendra Makanji from Haringey and Councillor Nirmal Roy from Camden. These Councillors guided and shaped the convention event itself. The workshop topics were all decided·by the councillors as key issues for Black, Asian and ethnic minority councillors and the community at large. The steering group members chaired the workshops and prepared the relevant material for the participants.

Our key speakers, Congressman Victor Frazer, Keith Vaz MP and Diane Abbott MP made the convention such a special occasion with their unique contributions. Herman Ouseley (Chair of the Commission for Racial Equality) reported back the key points from the workshops and summed up with the challenges ahead.

The support and interest shown to us by the United States Congressional Black Caucus was overwhelming.

Issue Communications, especially Sue Sansome, assisted in the organisational arrangements for the day and ensured that the event ran smoothly.

Natalie Demetrious from Lewisham Council compiled the list of the 450 Black, Asian and ethnic minority councillors around the country.

A special thank you to Councillor Sohpal and Claire Muir for all the work on the survey of councillors experiences.

We must also acknowledge the support that the Local Authority Associations, the Association of London Authorities, the Association of District Councils, the Association of Metropolitan Authorities, the Association of County Councils and the Convention of Scottish Local Authorities in writing to all leaders and chief executives to secure support for the convention.

A number of businesses also gave financial and support 'in kind': Coopers and Lybrand, Ashurst Morris Crisp, British Airways, the Edwardian Hotel and Dine Bangladeshi.

The Local Government Management Board, the

Local Government Information Unit, the Commission for Racial Equality, the London Labour Party, CVS Services and Unison also contributed financially to the Convention.

Thanks also to Neil Pollard for the design and production of publicity materials for the convention and for the typesetting and design of this report.

The final report has been prepared by Darryl Telles and Munira Thobani from Hounslow Council.

The Local Government Information Unit and Hansib Publications have together financed the publication.

Our final thanks go to Hounslow Leisure Services and the House of Commons for the entertainment and hospitality given to the speakers and all the delegates. We were very pleased to have Simon Hughes MP and Baroness Flather as our key speakers at the House of Commons.

All these people contributed money, time and enthusiasm which ensured that the Convention was a huge success.

Appendix
List of Delegates

Bedford BC
Apu Bagchi
Muhammad Khan
Sesa Lehal

Bedfordshire
M.R. Ali
Norris Bullock
Jim Thakoordin
Mohamad Yasin

Berkshire
Paul Sohal
Mohammad Iqbal
Mohammed Khan

Birmingham City
Mahtab Khan (Officer)
Henry Coore, Asst.
Director, Equal Opps.
Bill Doyle
Sybil Spence
Phil Murphy
Dorothy Wallace
Muhammad Afzal

Blackburn Borough
M. Khan

Bolton MBC
Campbell Benjamin

Bradford City
Mohammed Ajeeb

L.B. Brent
Bertha Joseph
Bobby Thomas
Jan Etienne
Colum Moloney

Bristol City
Haroun Saad

Buckinghamshire
Chester Jones

L.B. Camden
Nirmal Roy
S. Deshmukh
Jerry Williams

Cambridgeshire
Ansar Ali
Bachan Bhalla
Harmesh Lakhanpaul

Cardiff City
Harry Ernest

Cherwell District
Mrs. S. Deshi

Coventry City
S.S. Bains
M. Asif
J.S. Birdi
P.L. Joshi
R.S. Kanwar
R.P. Lakha

L.B. Croydon
Raj Chandarana
Clarence McKenzie
C. Bernard
Shafi Khan

Derby City
Ashok Kalia
Fareed Hussain
Abdul Rehman

Derbyshire County
Masud Akhtar
Hardyal Dhindsa

Darlington
R. Francis

Dudley
Mushtaq Hussain

L.B. Ealing
Jasbinder Birk

L.B. Enfield
Cllr George Savva
Mrs Yasmin Brett

L.B. Greenwich
Claudia Slee
K. Dhillon
Jagir K. Sekhon
Samuel Coker
Kanta Patel
Claude Ramsey

Hamilton District
Mushtaq Ahmad

L.B. H'smith & Fulham
Lester Holloway
Nadeem Aftab
Gerald Johnson
Jafar Khaled

L.B. Harrow
Mrs L Champagnie
Navin Shah
Mrs N Boethe

L.B. Hackney
Ken Hanson
Josh Lamb
Bill O'Connor
Saleem Siddiqui

Cynthia Thomas
O'Garrow
Cllr Momodu-Sillah

L.B. Haringey
Rahman Khan
E. Prescott
E. Dickerson
B. Sisupalan
A. Zaman
D. Basu
M. Appadoo
R. Mughal
N. Makanji
J. Patel
M. Lambie
I. Diakides

Harlow District
Feroz Khan

Hampshire County
K. P. Jessavala

Hertfordshire
Michael Blackman

L.B. Hillingdon
Dalip Chand
Gulab Sharma

L.B. Hounslow
G. Agarwal(Mayor)
R. Bath
M. Chaudhary
A. Dhillon
M. Gill
S. Jassar
I. Khwaja

T. Louki
A. Mann
J. Sharma
J. Singh
Peter Smith
Paul Tomlin

L.B. Islington
J. Winston
M. Babulall
T. Karim
P. Munim
R. McKenzie

R.B. Kensington & Chelsea
Joanna Edward

R.B. Kingston
Rajendra Pandya

Kirklees MBC
Dr. H.T. Gowda
Jamil Akhtar

Lancashire County
M.A. Umerji

Leeds City
Norma Hutchinson
Alison Lowe

Leicester City
Joe Allen

Leicestershire
Abdul R. Osman

L.B. Lewisham
M.L. Ng
M. Mohan

M. Iloghalu
F. Hayee
A. Arain
J. Parmar
S. Brown
E. Capone
T. Oke
C. Gonsalves
L. Eytle
S. Padmore
A. Simpson
O. Adefiranye

Luton Borough
S. Knight
Masood Akhtar

Manchester MDC
Tutu Eko
Vince Young
Yomi Mambu
George Harding
Nilofar Siddiqi

Middlesbrough BC
Ashok Kumar

Newcastle upon Tyne
Sajawal Khan

L.B. Newham
Murtland Inveraray
Mahmood Ahmad
Shama Ahmad
Mian Aslam
Akbar Chaudhary
Bashir-Ul Hafeez
Anand Patel

Northamptonshire
Chaman Kalyan

Nottinghamshire
Eunice Campbell
M. Riasat

Oxford City
Robert Evans

Oxfordshire County
S. Deshi

Reading Borough
Raj Sohpal

L.B. Redbridge
Asaf B. Mirza

Rochdale
Abdul H Chowdry JP

Rotherham
N. Ahmed

St Albans City
Khalil R. Moghul

Sheffield City
I.M. Walayat

Slough Borough
Cllr Dosanjh
Cllr Lodhi
Cllr Mann
Cllr Ghatora

Southampton
Jim Baker
Paramjit Bahia

South Tyneside
Syed Faruk Hussain

L.B. Southwark
Abdul-Rahman
O. Olayiwola
Hassan Vahib
Sonia Murison
Harry Canagasabey
Cecile Lothian

Staffordshire
Mr. & Mrs. A.R.
Hanchard
Mr. Nadir Imamoglu

Strathclyde
Mrs Neelam Bakshi

**South Glamorgan
County**
Ben Foday

Thamesdown BC
Bert Smith

Three Rivers DC
Glyn Abraham

L.B. Tower Hamlets
Abdul Shukir
Nooruddin Ahmed
Sunahwar Ali
Bodrul Alom
Soyful Alom
Rajan Uddin Jalal
J. Ramanoop
M.S. Uddin

L.B. Waltham Forest
L. Ali
N. Matharoo

Warwickshire
Mota Singh

Watford Borough
Rabi Martins
J. Dhindsa

Welwyn Hatfield
Kumar Sandy

W. Glamorgan
M. Verma

Wiltshire County
Andrew Edwards

Wolverhampton BC
M. Jaspal
T. Singh
L. Turner

Wycombe District
Sebert H. Graham
Cllr Razzaq

*Attending the convention
in individual capacity:*
Mrs. Neetinder Boparai
from North London.
David Forbes
of PRAXIS.
Ms. Esther Persaud from
L.B. Wandsworth.